The Ultimate Guide to Brand Archetypes for Business Strategies

Copyright © 2024 Reginaldo Osnildo
All rights reserved.

- PRESENTATION 4
- INTRODUCTION TO BRAND ARCHETYPES 7
- THE PSYCHOLOGY BEHIND ARCHETYPES 11
- IDENTIFYING YOUR BRAND ARCHETYPE 15
- THE 12 MAIN ARCHETYPES 19
- ARCHETYPE AND BRAND IDENTITY 25
- ARCHETYPE AND BRAND COMMUNICATION 29
- DEVELOPING A CONSISTENT BRAND VOICE 33
- ARCHETYPE AND CUSTOMER EXPERIENCE 37
- USING ARCHETYPES FOR MARKET DIFFERENTIATION .. 41
- BRAND ARCHETYPE AND NARRATIVE 45
- MEASURING BRAND ARCHETYPE EFFICACY 49
- ADAPTATION OF THE ARCHETYPE OVER TIME 53
- ARCHETYPES IN DIFFERENT CULTURES 57
- AVOIDING COMMON TRAPS WITH ARCHETYPES 61
- CASE STUDIES OF SUCCESSFUL BRAND ARCHETYPES ... 65
- ARCHETYPES AND DIGITAL MARKETING 69
- ARCHETYPE AND STRATEGIC DECISIONS 74
- DEVELOPING ARCHETYPE-BASED MARKETING CAMPAIGNS 78
- ARCHETYPES AND CONSUMPTION TRENDS 82

INTEGRATION OF ARCHETYPES WITH PRODUCT STRATEGY 86

CUSTOMER FEEDBACK AND ARCHETYPES 90

TEAM BUILDING AND ARCHETYPES 94

ARCHETYPES IN ADVERTISING 98

WORKSHOPS AND TRAININGS ON ARCHETYPES 102

IMPLEMENTING A WINNING ARCHETYPE STRATEGY .. 107

CHECKLIST FOR EVALUATION OF ARCHETYPES IN EXISTING BUSINESSES 111

60-DAY ACTION PLAN FOR IMPLEMENTING ARCHETYPES IN NEW BUSINESSES 115

REGINALDO OSNILDO 120

PRESENTATION

Welcome to the world of brand archetypes, where ancient wisdom meets modern business strategy. You are about to embark on a transformative journey with the book **"The Definitive Guide to Brand Archetypes for Business Strategy"** . This book is not just a manual, it is a portal to deeply understand how to connect your brand in an authentic and powerful way with your audience.

As an entrepreneur or marketer, you know that building a strong brand doesn't happen by accident. It's the result of strategic decisions and precise communication. Brand archetypes offer a path to achieving this precision, creating an identity that truly resonates with the needs and desires of consumers.

This book was created to be the most comprehensive resource on the market on the strategic use of archetypes in branding. In it, you will find everything from fundamental theory to practical applications that will transform your business approach. By applying the insights presented here, you will be able to align your brand message, differentiate yourself in the market, and create lasting connections with your audience.

Throughout the chapters, you'll be guided through a detailed exploration of each archetype, learning how to identify the archetype that best represents your brand, and how to integrate this understanding into every aspect of your business strategy. Each chapter is designed to be self-contained, providing not only knowledge, but also practical actions and reflections that will ensure you're always one step ahead.

Get ready to transform your brand's identity and communication with the power of archetypes. By the end of this book, you will not only understand archetypes, but you will also know how to use them to speak directly to the heart of your audience, ensuring a brand that is not only remembered, but truly felt.

Yours sincerely

Reginaldo Osnildo

INTRODUCTION TO BRAND ARCHETYPES

As you begin your journey into the world of brand archetypes, you are preparing to unlock one of the most powerful tools in the modern branding arsenal. This chapter provides an overview of what archetypes are, why they are relevant to building a strong brand, and how they can make a difference in your communication.

WHAT ARE ARCHETYPES?

Archetypes are essentially universal characters that reside in the collective unconscious. They represent fundamental patterns of behavior and narratives that are instantly recognizable and understandable across cultures and generations. Carl Jung, the renowned Swiss psychologist, introduced the idea that archetypes form the basis of the collective unconscious, making them common elements in all human stories and mythologies.

In the context of branding, archetypes are used to personify the brand in a way that resonates with fundamental human emotions and experiences. When a brand adopts an archetype, it is not just choosing a character for its narrative; it is aligning with a set of values, behaviors, and expectations that already exist in the minds of its audience.

WHY ARE ARCHETYPES IMPORTANT FOR BRANDS?

You may be wondering why you should consider archetypes in your branding strategy. The answer is simple: archetypes create a deep emotional connection.

They are powerful tools for humanizing your brand, making it more relatable and trustworthy. By choosing an appropriate archetype, your brand can:

- **Establish a clear identity:** Archetypes help define who your brand is at the most fundamental level. This not only simplifies communication, but also helps consumers quickly understand what your brand stands for.

- **Differentiate yourself from the competition:** In a saturated market, archetypes offer a clear way to stand out by showcasing what makes your brand unique.

- **Build consistency:** When all your communications and interactions are aligned with a specific archetype, your brand becomes more consistent. This reinforces brand identity and increases consumer loyalty.

- **Generate greater engagement:** Archetypes speak directly to people's fundamental desires and fears, which can make your marketing more impactful and memorable.

HOW ARE ARCHETYPES USED IN BRAND STRATEGIES?

Implementing archetypes into your brand strategy isn't just about choosing a character or persona that you like. It's a strategic decision that should reflect your company's core values, your target audience's expectations, and your brand's long-term goals. Throughout this book, you'll learn how to identify the archetype that best aligns with your brand and how to apply it effectively across all facets of your communications.

THE PSYCHOLOGY BEHIND ARCHETYPES

Now that you understand what archetypes are and why they're so important to building a strong brand, it's time to explore the psychology behind them. This chapter dives into the psychological roots of archetypes, explaining how they influence consumer behavior and why they're such a powerful tool in brand communication.

PSYCHOLOGICAL FUNDAMENTALS OF ARCHETYPES

Archetypes have their roots in Carl Jung's concept of the collective unconscious, which proposed that there is a set of memories and ideas shared across all human cultures. These ideas, or archetypes, are manifestations of universal human experiences. In marketing, by invoking these archetypes, brands can tap into deep and resonant emotions.

The psychology of archetypes shows that people tend to attribute human characteristics to objects and entities, including brands. This process, known as anthropomorphization, helps consumers better understand and emotionally connect with brands, which is essential for building lasting relationships and loyalty.

ARCHETYPES AND CONSUMER BEHAVIOR

Understanding how archetypes influence consumer behavior is crucial to effectively applying them to your brand strategy. Each archetype evokes specific sets of values and qualities that resonate with different audiences. For example:

- **The Hero:** inspires admiration and aspiration; is attractive to consumers who value courage, perseverance and achievement.

- **The Caregiver:** evokes empathy and protection; appeals to those who value nurturing, caring and generosity.

- **The Explorer:** encourages discovery and adventure; attracts consumers seeking freedom and new experiences.

By choosing an archetype that aligns with your brand's core values and your target audience's expectations, you can create messages that not only capture attention, but also drive action and loyalty.

APPLYING ARCHETYPAL PSYCHOLOGY IN PRACTICE

Applying archetypal psychology to your brand strategy shouldn't be haphazard. It requires a deep understanding of both the archetype and your target audience. Here are some best practices for integrating archetypes into your brand strategy:

- **Target audience analysis:** Understand who your consumers are and what they value. This will help determine which archetype your brand should embody.

- **Consistency in communication:** All your brand messages should be filtered through your chosen archetype. This ensures that every customer touchpoint reinforces your brand's archetypal identity.

- **Stories that resonate:** Use stories that exemplify the traits of your brand archetype to create an engaging and memorable narrative.

- **Feedback and adaptation:** Monitor how your audience responds to the chosen archetype and be ready to adjust your approach if necessary.

By mastering the psychology of archetypes, you will be well equipped to use these powerful psychological tools to strengthen your brand and deepen your connection with your customers.

IDENTIFYING YOUR BRAND ARCHETYPE

After exploring the importance of archetypes and how they affect consumer psychology, the next step is to identify which archetype best aligns with your brand's essence. This chapter provides a step-by-step guide to help you discover the archetype that encapsulates your company's values, mission, and vision, ensuring that your brand identity is both authentic and impactful.

STEP 1: UNDERSTANDING YOUR BRAND VALUES

Before choosing an archetype, it's crucial to have a clear understanding of your brand's core values. Ask yourself:

- What are my company's guiding principles?

- What does my brand represent?

- What promises does my brand make to its customers?

These questions will help outline your brand's moral and ethical character, which are essential to choosing the right archetype.

STEP 2: ANALYZING THE MISSION AND VISION

Your company's mission and vision are also critical components of identifying your archetype. They define your brand's purpose and aspirations, respectively, and should align with your chosen archetype. If your brand's mission is to inspire and empower, archetypes like the Hero or the Magician might be a good fit.

STEP 3: ASSESSING BRAND PERSONALITY

Consider your brand's personality as if it were a person. What kind of personality traits does your brand display? Is your brand more serious or playful? Conservative or innovative? Answering these questions can help you identify which archetype best aligns with how your brand presents itself to the world.

STEP 4: ALIGNING WITH MARKETING OBJECTIVES

Your marketing goals should also influence your choice of archetype. For example, if your goal is to build trust and confidence in a new market, the Caregiver might be the ideal archetype. If you want to highlight innovation and creativity, the Creator or Magician might be more appropriate.

STEP 5: USING TOOLS AND RESOURCES

There are several tools and resources that can assist in this process, including:

- **Branding workshops:** Collaborative sessions that help the team explore and define the archetypal aspects of the brand.

- **Consumer surveys:** Getting direct feedback from consumers can reveal how they perceive the brand, which can help identify the archetype that is already being projected.

- **Competitive analysis:** Understanding how competitors position their brands can offer insights into potentially underutilized or saturated archetypes in the market.

STEP 6: DECISION AND IMPLEMENTATION

After carrying out this comprehensive analysis, the next step is to consciously decide on the archetype that best represents your brand. This is a crucial moment, as it will define how the brand communicates and positions itself in the market.

Correctly identifying your brand archetype is not just a theoretical exercise; it is a strategy that can set the tone for all your marketing and communication actions. By choosing an archetype that truly resonates with your brand's values and personality, you establish a solid foundation for building an authentic and engaging narrative.

THE 12 MAIN ARCHETYPES

Now that you know how to identify the archetype that best aligns with your brand, let's take a deeper dive into each of the 12 core archetypes. This chapter will detail the characteristics, associated values, and examples of brands that exemplify each archetype. Understanding each archetype in depth will help you implement this powerful branding tool effectively and authentically.

1 - THE INNOCENT

- **Values:** Purity, optimism, simplicity.

- **Example brands:** Dove, Coca-Cola.

- **Application:** Ideal for brands that want to convey confidence and optimism, promoting simple and pure products.

2 - THE WISE MAN

- **Values:** Wisdom, knowledge, authority.

- **Example brands:** Google, BBC.

- **Application:** Perfect for brands that position themselves as sources of reliable information and want to promote education and knowledge.

3 - THE EXPLORER

- **Values:** Independence, adventure, free spirit.

- **Example brands:** Jeep, Red Bull.

- **Application:** Great for brands that promote active lifestyles or products that encourage discovery and adventure.

4 - THE OUTLAW

- **Values:** Rebellion, freedom, revolution.

- **Example brands:** Harley-Davidson, Virgin.

- **Application:** Suitable for brands that challenge the status quo and appeal to consumers who value individuality and freedom.

5 - THE WIZARD

- **Values:** Transformation, inspiration, mysticism.

- **Example brands:** Disney, Apple.

- **Application:** Ideal for brands that aim to create experiences that transform the usual reality and promote magic and enchantment.

6 - THE HERO

- **Values:** Courage, perseverance, heroism.

- **Example brands:** Nike, Adidas.

- **Application:** Excellent for brands associated with sports and challenges, promoting overcoming and achievement.

7 - THE LOVER

- **Values:** Passion, pleasure, connection.

- **Example brands:** Victoria's Secret , Alfa Romeo.

- **Application:** Perfect for brands that focus on creating emotional connections by offering luxurious or romantic products.

8 - THE COURT JOLLY

- **Values:** Humor, fun, irreverence.

- **Example brands:** M&M's , Old Spice.

- **Application:** Ideal for brands that want to be seen as sources of joy and fun, attracting consumers through humor and lightness.

9 - THE CAREGIVER

- **Values:** Altruism, care, protection.

- **Example brands:** Johnson & Johnson, TOMS.

- **Application:** Suitable for brands that emphasize care and support, whether in health products or social initiatives.

10 - THE RULER

- **Values:** Control, stability, leadership.

- **Example brands:** Mercedes-Benz, Microsoft.

- **Application:** Perfect for brands that position themselves as market leaders, offering products or services that promote stability and security.

11 - THE CREATOR

- **Values:** Innovation, creativity, originality.

- **Example brands:** LEGO, Adobe.

- **Application:** Ideal for brands that value creativity and innovation, offering products that allow personal expression and creation.

12 - THE COMMON

- **Values:** Honesty, simplicity, realism.

- **Example brands:** IKEA, Wrangler.

- **Application:** Great for brands that pride themselves on being approachable and trustworthy, attracting consumers who value authenticity and simplicity.

Each archetype has a unique set of characteristics and values that, when aligned with your brand's, can significantly amplify your brand's emotional resonance and customer loyalty. Choosing the right archetype not only allows you to differentiate your brand in the marketplace, but also establish a deeper connection with your consumers.

ARCHETYPE AND BRAND IDENTITY

Once you have a clear understanding of the 12 core archetypes and identified which one best represents your brand, it is crucial to integrate this archetype into your brand identity. This chapter will detail how you can weave your chosen archetype into the different elements that make up your brand identity, from visual design to tone of voice, ensuring a coherent and compelling presentation.

INTEGRATING THE ARCHETYPE INTO VISUAL DESIGN

Your brand's visual identity is often the first interaction consumers have with your company. For your chosen archetype to be effective, it must be clearly reflected in your design, including your logo, color palette, typography, and imagery. For example:

- **The Hero:** You can use strong, vibrant colors like red and black, with images of people overcoming challenges.

- **The Lover:** Prefers warm, sensual colors like pink and red, with soft, curved fonts.

Each choice must reinforce the characteristics of the archetype, conveying the values and essence of the brand in a visually impactful way.

ARCHETYPE IN TONE OF VOICE

Your brand's tone of voice is crucial to communicating your archetype consistently. This tone should be adapted to reflect the archetype's qualities across all communication channels, from advertisements to customer service interactions. For example:

> **- The Sage:** Uses an informative and authoritative tone, offering knowledge and advice.
>
> **- The Court Jester:** Adopts a lighter and more humorous style, often using wordplay or jokes.

Consistency in tone of voice not only strengthens brand identity, but also helps build trust and loyalty among consumers.

CONSISTENCY ACROSS CHANNELS

Maintaining consistency of the archetype across all channels is key. This includes digital marketing, advertising, packaging, and even the user experience online and in-store. Each touchpoint is an opportunity to reinforce the brand archetype and deepen the connection with the audience.

> **- Online:** Websites and social networks that visually and textually reflect the chosen archetype.
>
> **- Physical stores:** The environment must evoke the values of the archetype, whether through the layout, decoration or even customer service.

EVALUATION AND ADJUSTMENT

Implementing an archetype into your brand identity is an ongoing process. It's essential to regularly assess how your audience is responding and adjust elements as needed to maintain brand relevance and effectiveness. Tools like customer satisfaction surveys, social media analytics, and direct feedback can be invaluable for this fine-tuning.

Integrating a chosen archetype into your brand identity isn't a one-time project; it's a vital, ongoing element of your brand strategy. By ensuring that every aspect of your brand—from visualization to voice—is aligned with the archetype, you'll lay a solid foundation for a brand identity that not only stands out in the marketplace, but also resonates deeply with your consumers.

ARCHETYPE AND BRAND COMMUNICATION

Now that you've integrated the archetype into your brand identity, it's essential to align your marketing communications with that same archetype to maintain consistency and effectiveness. This chapter will discuss how you can apply your chosen archetype to your communications strategies, ensuring that each message reinforces your brand identity and resonates with your target audience.

DEFINING COMMUNICATION STRATEGIES

The first step to aligning your brand communication with the archetype is to clearly define the strategies you will use. This includes choosing the appropriate channels, messaging style, and type of content you will distribute. For example:

- **For the Explorer archetype:** Use communications that encourage adventure and discovery. Social media campaigns can feature exotic destinations or challenging activities to attract your audience.

- **For the Caregiver archetype:** Messages across all channels should emphasize safety, care, and support, using language that communicates empathy and protection.

ALIGNING THE MESSAGE WITH THE ARCHETYPE

Every piece of communication should be filtered through the archetype to ensure that the message is not only consistent but also strengthens the emotional connection with the audience. This includes advertising, PR, online content, email marketing and even packaging and merchandising. Messages should reflect the values and essence of the archetype in a clear and understandable way.

CREATIVITY AND INNOVATION IN COMMUNICATION

While consistency is vital, it's also important to remain creative in your communications. This keeps your audience engaged and allows your brand to stand out in a competitive market. For example:

- **Innovating with the Wizard:** Campaigns that use augmented or virtual reality to create magical and transformative experiences can effectively capture the audience's imagination.

- **Humor with the Court Jester:** Ads that use humor, wordplay or comical situations can create a memorable and accessible brand.

CONSISTENCY ACROSS PLATFORMS

Consistency is key to brand building. Make sure every campaign, social media post, email, or promotional material aligns with your chosen archetype. Consistency creates a strong, trustworthy brand, while inconsistency can confuse and alienate your audience.

EVALUATION AND REVIEW

Monitoring and evaluating the effectiveness of your brand communications is crucial. Use data analytics, customer feedback, and engagement metrics to understand what's working and what can be improved. This ongoing review process will help keep your communications fresh and relevant.

Aligning your marketing communications with your brand archetype isn't just about maintaining consistency; it's about creating an authentic, engaging voice that speaks directly to the hearts and minds of consumers. When executed well, the archetype can completely transform the public's perception of your brand, building loyalty and differentiating your offering in a crowded marketplace.

DEVELOPING A CONSISTENT BRAND VOICE

Your brand voice is one of the most critical elements in building a coherent and memorable brand identity. This chapter focuses on how you can use your chosen archetype to develop a brand voice that is not only consistent, but also captivates and engages your audience in an authentic and lasting way.

THE IMPORTANCE OF BRAND VOICE

Brand voice is the verbal expression of your brand's personality. It influences how your brand communicates in everything from advertising campaigns to social media posts, emails, and internal communications. A consistent brand voice helps build recognition and trust with your audience, while an inconsistent voice can confuse and alienate consumers.

ALIGNING THE VOICE WITH THE ARCHETYPE

Each archetype has unique characteristics that should be reflected in your brand voice:

- **The Creator:** Inspiring and innovative, focused on showing novelty and possibility.

- **The Ruler:** Authoritative and confident, conveying a sense of leadership and stability.

- **The Lover:** Sensual and engaging, creating an atmosphere of intimacy and connection.

For each archetype, think about the voice qualities that best represent your essence and how these qualities can be expressed verbally.

PRACTICAL EXAMPLES OF BRAND VOICE

- **For the Explorer:** Use a voice that encourages adventure and freedom. Your texts should inspire people to explore the unknown, with phrases that evoke a sense of travel and discovery.

- **For the Caregiver:** The voice should be warm and protective, with language that conveys care and support, often using terms that express safety and comfort.

CONSISTENCY ACROSS ALL CHANNELS

To maintain brand voice consistency:

- **Document voice guidelines:** Create a style guide that clearly defines how your brand voice should be applied in different contexts.

- **Train your team:** Make sure everyone involved in brand communication understands and can apply the brand voice effectively.

- **Review regularly:** As your brand evolves, revisit and adjust your brand voice as needed to ensure it remains relevant and effective.

MEASURING THE EFFICACY OF BRAND VOICE

Use customer feedback, social media engagement analytics, and other performance metrics to assess the effectiveness of your brand voice. This not only helps you understand what resonates with your audience, but also points out areas for adjustments and improvements.

Developing and maintaining a consistent brand voice is essential to any successful brand strategy. By aligning this voice with your chosen archetype, your brand will not only speak more clearly and persuasively, but it will also establish a stronger emotional connection with your audience. Your brand voice is a powerful storytelling tool that, when used correctly, can set your brand apart in today's competitive marketplace.

ARCHETYPE AND CUSTOMER EXPERIENCE

Integrating your brand archetype into your customer experience is essential to creating a cohesive, engaging interaction that reflects your brand identity and strengthens your connection with your audience. This chapter explores how you can weave your chosen archetype into every customer touchpoint, from first engagement to after-sales service, ensuring a memorable experience that aligns with your brand values.

UNDERSTANDING CUSTOMER EXPERIENCE

Customer experience encompasses all aspects of your audience's interaction with your brand, including advertising, purchasing, product or service usage, and support. A well-designed, consistent experience can turn casual customers into brand advocates, while negative or inconsistent experiences can damage perception and loyalty.

INCORPORATING THE ARCHETYPE AT EACH STAGE

- **Discovery and awareness:** At the beginning of the customer journey, where they discover your brand, use the archetype to tell a story that captures attention and sparks interest. For example, an Explorer archetype could be presented through campaigns that highlight adventure and discovery.

- **Consideration and purchase:** When customers are considering your offering, reinforce the archetype through marketing messages that highlight the brand's core values and qualities. For example, a Caregiver archetype can be emphasized through product guarantees and promises of excellent customer service.

- **Usage and experience:** During the use of the product or service, make sure that the archetype is present in elements such as design, functionality and user interaction. A Creator archetype, for example, can be expressed in products that encourage personalization and creativity.

- **Support and after-sales:** Customer service should reflect the archetype to ensure a consistent experience. For example, a Ruler archetype might ensure customer support that stands out for its authority, reliability, and efficiency.

STRATEGIES FOR EFFECTIVE IMPLEMENTATION

- **Team training:** Ensure that all staff, especially customer service staff, have a deep understanding of the brand archetype so that they can act in alignment with it in all interactions.

- **Feedback and adjustments:** Use customer feedback to continually adjust the experience, ensuring that the archetype is presented effectively and that all interactions reinforce the brand identity.

- **Monitoring and evaluation:** Regularly review and evaluate how the archetype is being integrated into the customer experience, using satisfaction and engagement metrics to guide improvements.

Integrating your chosen archetype into every step of the customer experience not only enriches that experience, but also strengthens your brand identity and cohesion. By ensuring that every interaction reflects the values and qualities of your archetype, you can create a deeper, more lasting relationship with your customers.

USING ARCHETYPES FOR MARKET DIFFERENTIATION

Market differentiation is key in a competitive landscape. Archetypes, when used strategically, can be a powerful tool to differentiate your brand from competitors. This chapter explores how you can use your chosen archetype to create a unique identity that not only sets your brand apart, but also effectively attracts and retains customers.

UNDERSTANDING MARKET DIFFERENTIATION

Market differentiation means establishing your brand as unique from competitors by highlighting features and benefits that only your brand can offer. Using archetypes helps you achieve this by giving your brand a distinct and memorable personality that resonates on an emotional level with your audience.

DIFFERENTIATION STRATEGIES USING ARCHETYPES

- **Archetype-Based Positioning:** Choose an archetype that not only aligns with your brand's vision and mission, but also stands out from those used by your competitors. For example, if most brands in your industry embrace the "Ruler" archetype, embracing the "Outlaw" archetype can help set your brand apart as a unique and compelling alternative.

- **Aligned communication and marketing:** Use the archetype to guide all your communication and marketing strategies. This includes the tone of your advertising campaigns, the aesthetics of your social media content, and the style of your customer service interactions. This consistency helps reinforce your unique brand identity and deepen your emotional connection with your audience.

- Personalized customer experiences: Create customer experiences that reflect your chosen archetype. For example, a brand that embraces the "Maker" archetype might offer product or service customization workshops that encourage creative expression from customers.

- Engaging brand stories: Use archetype-based storytelling to tell stories that capture the imagination and hearts of your audience. Stories that are consistent with your brand archetype tend to be more engaging and memorable.

BENEFITS OF DIFFERENTIATION THROUGH ARCHETYPES

- Emotional connection: Archetypes facilitate a deep emotional connection with the audience, which is essential for brand loyalty.

- Brand recognition: A brand that consistently communicates its archetype becomes easily recognizable and distinct.

- Consumer preference: Brands that stand out in their market and resonate emotionally with consumers tend to be preferred over less distinct competitors.

MONITORING AND ADAPTATION

It's crucial to monitor the effectiveness of your differentiation strategies to ensure they remain relevant and impactful. Pay attention to market feedback and be ready to adapt your approach if brand perception changes or new competitors emerge.

Using archetypes for market differentiation not only helps you establish a unique and compelling brand, but it also creates a sustainable competitive advantage. By delving into the unique qualities of your chosen archetype and integrating them into every aspect of your brand, you can ensure that your company stands out in a crowded market.

BRAND ARCHETYPE AND NARRATIVE

Narratives are essential to building strong brands; they tell the story of who you are, what you value, and why your customers should care. Integrating your chosen archetype into your brand narratives can transform the way you communicate with your audience, creating stories that not only capture attention but also inspire loyalty and action. This chapter explores how to effectively weave your brand archetype into your narratives to maximize emotional impact and engagement.

FUNDAMENTALS OF BRAND STORYTELLING

Effective brand narratives must be authentic, coherent, and resonate emotionally with the audience. They are built around the brand archetype, which provides a consistent framework that guides how the story is told, what points are emphasized, and the overall tone of the message.

INCORPORATING THE ARCHETYPE INTO STORIES

- **Identify core themes:** Each archetype has distinctive themes and motivations. For example, the Hero archetype might focus on overcoming challenges and bravery, while the Sage might focus on knowledge and enlightenment. Identify these themes in your own brand and use them as the backbone of your stories.

- **Develop archetypal characters:** Characters who embody your brand's archetype can serve as heroes in your narratives. These characters should exemplify the values and qualities of the archetype, acting as brand ambassadors in the stories.

- **Structure stories for emotional resonance:** Craft your stories in a way that will generate an emotional response that aligns with the archetype. For example, a brand that uses the Caregiver archetype should create stories that highlight empathy, care, and community as key points.

EXAMPLES OF EFFECTIVE NARRATIVES

- **The Hero's Journey:** Brands that use the Hero archetype can tell stories of customers overcoming obstacles with the help of their products or services.

- **The Wisdom of the Sage:** Brands that identify with the Sage archetype can share insights and wisdom, educating their audience on relevant topics that reinforce their authority in the industry.

ENSURING CONSISTENCY ACROSS PLATFORMS

Maintain consistency in your narrative across all platforms and customer touchpoints, from digital marketing to direct interactions. This not only reinforces your brand identity, but also ensures that your brand story is understood and appreciated consistently.

EVALUATION AND ADAPTATION OF THE NARRATIVE

Regularly evaluate the impact of your brand narratives. Use customer feedback, engagement analytics, and performance metrics to adjust and improve your stories. This ongoing process helps keep your narratives fresh, relevant, and aligned with audience expectations and needs.

By deeply integrating your archetype into your brand narratives, you not only tell your company's story more effectively, but you also build an emotional connection that can elevate brand perception and loyalty. Well-told stories are incredibly powerful and can transform the way consumers view and interact with your brand.

MEASURING BRAND ARCHETYPE EFFICACY

Once you've integrated your brand archetype into all areas of your communication and storytelling, it's crucial to evaluate whether these strategies are truly strengthening your brand and effectively connecting with your audience. This chapter discusses how to measure the effectiveness of your brand archetype, the tools and techniques you can use to collect important data, and how to interpret that data to make strategic adjustments.

ESTABLISHING SUCCESS METRICS

Before you can measure the effectiveness of your brand archetype, you need to define which metrics are most relevant to your business goals. These might include:

- **Consumer engagement:** Measures such as time of interaction with the brand, frequency of purchase, and engagement on social networks.

- **Brand recognition:** Increased brand recall and recognition in market research.

- **Conversions and sales:** Changes in sales figures, subscriptions to services or participation in promotional events.

- **Customer loyalty:** Customer retention rates and loyalty program enrollments.

TOOLS FOR COLLECTING DATA

To effectively measure the effectiveness of your brand archetype, you can utilize a variety of tools:

- **Customer satisfaction surveys:** To obtain direct feedback on how consumers perceive the brand and its values.

- **Social media analytics software:** To monitor audience engagement and reaction to online marketing campaigns.

- **Google Analytics:** To track user behavior on the brand's website and measure conversions and referring traffic.

INTERPRETING THE DATA

Collecting data is only part of the process; interpreting it correctly is crucial to understanding whether the archetype is being effective. Analyze the data for trends and patterns that indicate both successes and areas for improvement. For example, a high engagement rate on content that reflects the brand archetype may indicate strong resonance, while negative or lukewarm feedback may suggest the need for adjustments in communication.

ADJUSTING THE STRATEGY

Based on the data collected and its analysis, you should be prepared to make strategic adjustments. This may include:

- **Refine the archetype's communication:** If certain aspects of the archetype aren't resonating, consider how you can adjust the narrative or presentation to better align with audience expectations.

- **Increase team training:** If your team is not communicating the archetype effectively through customer service or marketing, more training may be needed.

- **Innovate in products or services:** If the data shows that the market is responding positively to the archetype, it may be an opportunity to expand or innovate in product or service lines that reinforce this identity.

Measuring the effectiveness of your brand archetype is not a one-time event, but an ongoing process that should evolve with your brand strategy. By maintaining a consistent cycle of evaluation and adjustment, you can ensure that your archetype continues to serve as a strong pillar for brand identity and growth.

ADAPTATION OF THE ARCHETYPE OVER TIME

As your brand grows and the market evolves, you may need to adjust your brand archetype to maintain relevance and resonance with your audience. This chapter discusses the importance of adapting your archetype over time, identifying signs that indicate the need for change, and exploring strategies for implementing these adaptations effectively.

RECOGNIZING THE NEED FOR CHANGE

Changes in the market, target audience, or company itself may require you to reevaluate and potentially adjust your brand archetype. Here are some indicators that a change may be necessary:

- **Demographic changes:** Significant changes in your audience demographics may require a reconsideration of the archetype to ensure it still resonates with your core audience.

- **Market trends:** New trends or changes in the industry can make certain archetypes more or less relevant.

- **Customer feedback:** Regular customer feedback may indicate that the current archetype is no longer aligning with consumer expectations or needs.

- **Brand performance results:** A drop in brand performance indicators, such as engagement, loyalty or sales, may suggest that the archetype needs to be revised.

STRATEGIES FOR ADAPTATION OF ARCHETYPES

1 - Research and analysis: Before making any changes, conduct in-depth research to understand the forces that are shaping your audience's needs and preferences, as well as market dynamics.

2 - Co-creation workshops: Involving internal and external stakeholders in workshops can help identify which new archetype can best represent the brand in light of the changes observed.

3 - Market testing: Before fully implementing a new archetype, test it in smaller segments of the market to gauge audience response and make adjustments before wide-scale launch.

4 - Gradual update: Introduce changes gradually so as not to alienate your existing audience. This may include updating marketing messages, reviewing visual identity and readjusting communication strategies to reflect the new archetype smoothly and consistently.

COMMUNICATING CHANGES TO THE PUBLIC

Effectively communicating archetype changes to consumers is crucial. Ensure communications are clear about how and why the brand is evolving, and highlight the benefits these changes will bring to customers. Maintaining transparency will help maintain customer trust and loyalty during the transition period.

POST-ADAPTATION MONITORING

Once a new archetype has been implemented, it's vital to continue monitoring how it's being received by your audience. Continue to use performance analytics and customer feedback to adjust your strategy as needed, ensuring your brand remains aligned with consumer expectations and needs.

Adapting your brand archetype over time is an essential part of brand management. Keeping your archetype aligned with market changes and audience needs not only helps maintain brand relevance, but also strengthens your brand, enabling sustainable growth and greater connection with customers.

ARCHETYPES IN DIFFERENT CULTURES

As your brand expands globally, it's crucial to understand how brand archetypes are perceived in different cultural contexts. This chapter discusses the importance of adapting archetypes to align with the specific cultural nuances of each market, ensuring that your communication is effective and resonant across different regions of the world.

UNDERSTANDING CULTURAL VARIATION OF ARCHETYPES

Archetypes, although universal in essence, can have different connotations and meanings in different cultures. For example:

- **The Hero:** In Western cultures, the Hero is often seen as a courageous and daring savior. However, in some Eastern cultures, the concept of a hero may be more closely linked to wisdom and patience.

- **The Sage:** While in the West the Sage may be associated with a scholar or scientist, in Eastern cultures he may be closer to a monk or spiritual guru.

These differences can influence how archetypes should be presented and communicated in different markets to ensure they connect authentically and respectfully.

STRATEGIES FOR ADAPTATION ARCHETYPES IN GLOBAL MARKETS

- **In-depth cultural research:** Before entering a new market, conduct in-depth research to understand prevailing beliefs, values, and behaviors. This includes studying how traditional archetypes are perceived and what variations may be needed.

- **Local Consulting:** Work with cultural experts and local consultants to adapt the archetypes in ways that respect and resonate with the local culture. They can offer valuable insights that can prevent misunderstandings and miscommunication.

- **Market testing:** Implement market testing to assess how adaptations of the archetype are received by local audiences. Use feedback to adjust the approach before a large-scale launch.

- **Flexible communication:** Develop marketing materials and communications that can be easily adjusted for different markets. This includes having multiple versions of advertising campaigns that highlight different aspects of the archetype that are most relevant to each culture.

EXAMPLES OF CULTURAL ADAPTATION

- **Differentiated campaigns:** A global beverage brand might use the Explorer archetype to promote adventure and the unknown in the US, while in

Japan, the same archetype might focus more on harmony with nature and inner discovery.

- Product modification: Some brands adapt not only their communication but also their products to better reflect cultural values that resonate with certain archetypes in specific markets.

Adapting archetypes to different cultures is crucial to a brand's global success. Understanding and respecting cultural variations in archetype meanings can lead to more effective communication, increasing brand relevance and strengthening its connection with consumers around the world.

AVOIDING COMMON TRAPS WITH ARCHETYPES

Implementing brand archetypes, while powerful, can present significant challenges. This chapter identifies some of the most common pitfalls brands may encounter when utilizing archetypes and offers strategic guidance on how to avoid them, ensuring that using archetypes in your brand strategy is effective and beneficial.

PITFALL 1: INCONGRUENT CHOICE OF ARCHETYPES

- **Problem:** Choosing an archetype that doesn't align with the brand's real or perceived values can create a disconnect with the audience.

- **Solution:** Conduct a deep analysis of your brand identity and target audience values before selecting an archetype. Consider conducting brand workshops and market research to ensure that your archetype choice truly reflects your brand essence and resonates with your audience.

PITFALL 2: SUPERFICIALITY IN EXECUTION

- **Problem:** Applying an archetype superficially, without integrating it deeply into all aspects of the brand, can result in a strategy that feels forced or inauthentic.

- **Solution:** Develop a comprehensive plan to embed the archetype into all facets of the brand, including marketing, communications, customer experience, and internal culture. Ensure that all departments understand and can consistently apply the archetype across their operations.

PITFALL 3: LACK OF DIFFERENTIATION

- **Problem:** Using an archetype that is widely popular in the industry can make it difficult to differentiate your brand from the competition.

- **Solution:** Find unique ways to interpret or present the archetype that distinguish your brand. Consider combining elements from different archetypes or highlighting less explored aspects of the chosen archetype to create a unique identity.

PITFALL 4: RIGIDITY IN APPLICATION

- **Problem:** Taking a rigid and inflexible approach to the archetype can prevent the brand from evolving and responding to market changes.

- **Solution:** Maintain a flexible approach, allowing the archetype to evolve with the brand and the market. Conduct regular reviews of the archetype strategy and be open to adjustments based on market feedback and brand performance.

PITFALL 5: DISREGARDING CULTURAL DIFFERENCES

- **Problem:** Failing to adapt the archetype to different cultures can lead to messages that are misinterpreted or offensive in some markets.

- **Solution:** Investigate the cultural connotations of the archetype in different markets and adjust your communication to ensure it is appropriate and resonant in each cultural context. Work with local experts to adapt your strategy effectively.

Avoiding these pitfalls not only increases the effectiveness of your brand archetype implementation, but also protects your brand's integrity and reputation in the long run. By taking a deliberate and strategic approach, your brand can use archetypes to build a strong and meaningful connection with your audience, differentiating yourself in the marketplace in an authentic and impactful way.

CASE STUDIES OF SUCCESSFUL BRAND ARCHETYPES

Exploring case studies where brand archetypes have been successfully utilized can provide valuable insights and inspiration for implementing archetype strategies within your own brand. This chapter explores several examples of companies that have effectively aligned their archetypes with their brand strategies, resulting in market recognition, customer loyalty, and business growth.

CASE STUDY 1: NIKE – THE HERO

- **Archetype:** The Hero

- **Strategy:** Nike has embraced the Hero archetype, positioning its products as tools that help consumers overcome challenges and achieve excellence.

- **Execution:** With inspirational slogans like "Just Do It," Nike encourages its customers to "fight" for their personal and athletic goals, reinforcing the idea that anyone can be a hero in their own story.

- **Results:** The heroic approach helped Nike become a market leader in sports equipment, establishing a strong emotional connection with its audience, who see the brand as a motivator to achieve success.

CASE STUDY 2: APPLE – THE WIZARD

- **Archetype:** The Magician

- **Strategy:** Apple uses the Wizard archetype to present its products as revolutionary and capable of transforming people's daily lives.

- **Execution:** Innovative product launches, such as the iPhone and iPad, are presented as wizards, promising new experiences and possibilities that previously seemed impossible.

- **Results:** This positioning has helped Apple cultivate a loyal consumer base who anticipate each new release and see the brand as a symbol of innovation and transformation.

CASE STUDY 3: DOVE – THE CAREGIVER

- **Archetype:** The Caregiver

- **Strategy:** Dove embraces the Caregiver archetype, focusing on creating a positive body image and caring for natural beauty.

- **Execution:** The "Real Beauty " campaign celebrates diversity and authenticity, showcasing women of different ages, sizes and ethnicities, and emphasizing care and acceptance.

- **Results:** The campaign not only significantly increased Dove's visibility and sales, but also established the brand as an advocate for women's emotional and physical well-being.

CASE STUDY 4: RED BULL – THE EXPLORER

- **Archetype:** The Explorer

- **Strategy:** Red Bull adopts the Explorer archetype, promoting an adventurous and energetic lifestyle.

- **Execution:** The brand is known for sponsoring extreme sports and limit-pushing events, such as skydiving and adventure racing.

- **Results: This strategy solidifies** Red Bull's image as a drink for those seeking excitement and adventure, expanding its reach and appeal in the young and dynamic market.

These case studies demonstrate how effective use of archetypes can differentiate a brand and create deep connections with consumers. By choosing and implementing an archetype that authentically resonates with their values and aspirations, brands can significantly amplify their impact and success in the marketplace.

ARCHETYPES AND DIGITAL MARKETING

In today's digital era, where communication strategies are dominated by digital, understanding how to integrate brand archetypes into digital marketing campaigns is essential to engaging audiences effectively and memorably. This chapter discusses how archetypes can be used to enhance your brand's digital presence, improving engagement and conversion across multiple online platforms.

USING ARCHETYPES IN DIGITAL CONTENT

- **Blogs and articles:** Use your brand archetype to set the tone and style of your content. For example, a Sage archetype can be used to create content that educates and informs, establishing your brand as an authority on the topic.

- **Videos:** Videos are particularly effective at conveying emotionally engaging archetypes like the Hero or the Wizard. They can be used to tell stories that illustrate the customer journey or the innovation behind a product.

- **Infographics and data visualizations:** For brands that embrace the Sage archetype, infographics are excellent tools for sharing knowledge in an accessible and visually appealing way.

SOCIAL MEDIA ENGAGEMENT STRATEGIES

Social media presence is a critical area where the brand archetype must be consistently applied to effectively engage with audiences.

- **Personality in posts:** Social networks offer a platform to humanize the brand through the archetype. For example, a Jester archetype could be perfect for brands that want to connect with their audience through humor on platforms like Twitter or TikTok.

- **Interactivity:** Encourage interaction with the audience by using the archetype to shape responses and comments, which can help strengthen emotional connection and increase engagement.

- **Campaigns and promotions:** Develop campaigns that reflect the brand's archetype, such as challenges or quizzes that engage the public in a way that is aligned with the brand's personality.

OPTIMIZATION FOR SEO AND ARCHETYPES

Using archetypes in your SEO strategy can help attract the right type of traffic to your website.

- **Keywords and archetypes:** Integrate your brand archetype into your keywords to attract visitors who align with your brand values. For example, a brand that embraces the Explorer archetype might focus on terms related to adventure and discovery.

- **Archetype-aligned content:** Create content that is not only SEO-optimized but also reinforces your chosen archetype, helping to build a consistent narrative that improves user engagement and retention.

MEASURING THE IMPACT OF ARCHETYPE IN DIGITAL MARKETING

It is vital to measure how the use of archetypes is impacting your digital marketing strategy:

- **Engagement Analysis:** Monitor how different types of content aligned with the archetype are performing in terms of likes, shares and comments.

- **Conversions:** Track conversions that can be directly attributed to archetype-influenced campaigns to understand the ROI of these strategies.

- **User Feedback:** Collect and analyze user feedback on how the brand personality, shaped by the archetype, affects their perception and purchasing decisions.

Archetypes offer a rich opportunity to differentiate your brand in the digital space. By integrating your chosen archetype creatively and strategically into your digital marketing, you can significantly improve customer engagement and loyalty by establishing a strong and cohesive online presence.

ARCHETYPE AND STRATEGIC DECISIONS

Integrating the brand archetype into strategic business and marketing decisions not only reinforces brand coherence, but also guides product development, innovation, and go-to-market strategies in a way that resonates deeply with audiences. This chapter discusses how archetypes can guide strategic decisions, ensuring that a brand maintains a clear and distinctive direction.

INTEGRATING THE ARCHETYPE INTO BUSINESS STRATEGIES

- **Product development:** The brand archetype can significantly influence the features and functionality of products. For example, a brand that embraces the Creator archetype might focus on products that allow for customization or express creativity.

- **Market positioning:** Choosing an archetype affects how a brand positions itself in relation to its competitors. A Ruler archetype, for example, can lead a brand to seek a position of leadership and authority in its sector.

- **Innovation:** The archetype can inspire specific innovations that are aligned with the brand's personality. A brand that uses the Explorer archetype can invest in technologies that open new horizons for its consumers.

MARKETING DECISIONS INFLUENCED BY THE ARCHETYPE

- **Advertising campaigns:** Campaigns should reflect the archetype to strengthen the brand identity. The Caregiver archetype, for example, suggests campaigns that emphasize service, support, and community.

- **Customer Relationship:** The way a brand communicates and interacts with customers should be influenced by the archetype. A brand that chooses the Lover archetype will focus on creating deep emotional connections and personalized experiences.

- **Geographic expansion:** When entering new markets, the archetype can help determine the best entry strategies and cultural adaptation, ensuring that the brand is positively received in different cultural contexts.

USE OF ARCHETYPE IN CRISIS MANAGEMENT

In times of crisis, the brand archetype can provide guidance on how to respond in a way that is consistent with the brand's identity. For example, a brand that embraces the Hero archetype might approach a crisis with a proactive and courageous attitude, focusing on overcoming challenges and protecting its customers.

ASSESSING THE IMPACT OF STRATEGIC DECISIONS

To ensure that archetype-based decisions are delivering the desired results, it is essential to continually measure the impact of those decisions:

- **Performance Analysis:** Monitor specific KPIs related to new products, marketing campaigns, and market expansions to assess success.

- **Customer feedback:** Collecting and analyzing customer feedback can provide insights into how archetype-based initiatives are being perceived and what adjustments may be needed.

Archetypes are more than just a branding tool; they are a strategic element that can guide a wide variety of business and marketing decisions. By aligning these decisions with the chosen archetype, a brand can ensure not only consistency and authenticity, but also a competitive advantage in the marketplace.

DEVELOPING ARCHETYPE-BASED MARKETING CAMPAIGNS

Successful marketing campaigns don't just promote products or services, they also strengthen your brand identity and create an emotional connection with your audience. Using your brand archetype as the foundation for your campaigns can help you achieve these goals more effectively. This chapter explores how to plan and implement marketing campaigns that make the most of your chosen archetype, ensuring greater resonance and impact.

ARCHETYPE-BASED CAMPAIGN PLANNING

- **Goal Setting:** Align the campaign goals with the archetype's qualities. For example, if the archetype is the Explorer, the campaign might aim to increase the brand's perception as a leader in innovation and adventure.

- **Identifying the target audience:** Consider how the characteristics of the archetype resonate with your target audience. Tailor the message to meet the expectations and desires of that audience, using the archetype to shape that communication.

- **Messaging and content creation:** Develop messaging and content that exemplifies the archetype. For example, a brand that uses the Caregiver archetype should emphasize messages of support, care, and community in its campaigns.

CAMPAIGN EXECUTION

- **Choosing communication channels:** Select the channels that best align with the archetype and target audience. For example, if the archetype is the Court Jester, platforms like TikTok and Instagram may be ideal for humorous and visual campaigns.

- **Implementing creative strategies:** Utilize creative approaches that reflect the archetype in action. This can include everything from the visual style of advertisements to the type of events or promotions held.

- **Multichannel integration:** Make sure all campaign pieces across different channels are cohesive and consistently reinforce the archetype. Cohesion increases campaign effectiveness and strengthens brand identity.

MONITORING AND EVALUATION

- **Tracking and analytics:** Use monitoring tools to track campaign performance in real time. This includes analyzing engagement, reach, conversions, and other relevant metrics.

- **Consumer feedback:** Collect direct consumer feedback to understand how the campaign is being perceived and which aspects are most effectively communicating the archetype.

- **Real-time adjustments:** Be prepared to make adjustments during the campaign based on the data collected and feedback received to maximize effectiveness.

Developing marketing campaigns that are true to your brand archetype can transform how audiences perceive and interact with your brand. Archetype-based campaigns not only attract attention, but also create a memorable experience that can increase customer loyalty and engagement. Brands that understand how to apply their archetypes to marketing campaigns are better positioned to stand out in competitive markets.

ARCHETYPES AND CONSUMPTION TRENDS

Understanding and responding to consumer trends is crucial to the long-term success of any brand. By reflecting universal patterns of human behavior, archetypes can be valuable tools for predicting and responding to these trends. This chapter explores how archetypes can help you identify shifts in consumer preferences and how you can use them to effectively adapt your strategies.

UNDERSTANDING TRENDS THROUGH ARCHETYPES

- **Trend and archetype analysis:** Study how certain archetypes gain popularity in response to cultural, economic, and social changes. For example, in times of economic uncertainty, the Caregiver archetype may become more relevant, while in periods of optimism, the Explorer may prevail.

- **Consumer behavior prediction:** Use your understanding of archetypes to predict how consumer values and behaviors may change. This can help anticipate future demands and guide product and service development.

APPLYING ARCHETYPES TO MARKETING STRATEGIES

- **Product alignment with trends:** Adjust your brand's products and services to reflect archetypes that are on the rise. For example, if the Hero archetype is gaining traction, consider products that empower consumers to achieve their own heroic feats.

- **Adaptive campaigns:** Develop marketing campaigns that speak to emerging trends and resonate with the relevant archetype. This may include changing the messaging of existing campaigns or launching new initiatives that capitalize on changing consumer preferences.

STRATEGIC RESPONSE TO MARKET CHANGES

- **Flexibility and agility:** Maintain flexibility in your brand strategy to adapt quickly to changes. Companies that can pivot or adjust their approaches based on evolving consumer archetypes and trends are more likely to remain relevant and competitive.

- **Continuous consumer engagement:** Use surveys, focus groups, and social media feedback to maintain an open dialogue with consumers. This not only helps you better understand their needs and wants, but also reinforces their emotional connection with the brand.

MEASURING SUCCESS

- **Data analysis:** Use analytical tools to measure how adaptations based on archetypes and consumer trends are performing in terms of sales, engagement and brand recognition.

- **Performance-based adjustments:** Be prepared to continually make adjustments, based on hard data and market feedback, to ensure strategies remain effective and relevant.

Archetypes offer a powerful lens through which brands can interpret and respond to ever-changing consumer trends. By aligning marketing and product development strategies with relevant archetypes, brands can not only anticipate market needs but also deeply engage with their consumers, building a solid foundation for continued growth and success.

INTEGRATION OF ARCHETYPES WITH PRODUCT STRATEGY

Integrating archetypes into your product strategy is an effective way to ensure that your products or services resonate deeply with your target audience's values and expectations. This chapter details how archetypes can be used to guide product development from concept to launch, strengthening your brand's connection with its consumers.

ARCHETYPE-BASED PLANNING

- **Product goal setting:** Set clear goals for each new product or service based on the chosen archetype. For example, products created under the Creator archetype should encourage innovation and creative expression from users.

- **Aligned market research:** Conduct market research that considers how the archetype may influence consumer preferences and needs. This includes understanding the audience's emotional and practical expectations for products that align with a given archetype.

- **Guided product development:** Use the archetype to guide all phases of product development, from design to functionality to marketing messaging. This ensures that the final product not only meets market needs but also amplifies the brand identity.

PRODUCT STRATEGY EXECUTION

- **Design and packaging:** Make sure your product design and packaging clearly communicate the archetype. For example, a product that represents the Explorer archetype might feature packaging that suggests adventure and discovery, with vibrant colors and images of distant landscapes.

- **Launch communication:** Plan the product launch to reinforce the archetype through advertising campaigns, launch events and other promotional activities. The message should be consistent across all channels.

- **Customer Experience:** Provide a customer experience that is in harmony with the archetype. For example, if the archetype is the Caregiver, the post-sale experience should emphasize support and customer service, reinforcing the promise of care and attention.

MONITORING AND ADJUSTMENT

- **Continuous feedback:** Collect continuous feedback from customers on how they perceive and interact with the product. This is crucial to understanding whether the archetype integration is being effective.

- **Performance Analysis:** Monitor product performance in the market in terms of sales, customer satisfaction, and engagement. Use this data to make necessary adjustments to your product strategy.

- **Product iteration:** Based on feedback and performance analysis, iterate the product to better align with the archetype and market expectations. This may include changes to the design, functionality, or marketing strategy.

Integrating archetypes into product strategy isn't just about creating products that sell, it's about developing offerings that live and breathe the brand's values, creating a deep emotional resonance with audiences. By aligning product development with the brand archetype, companies can ensure that each product not only meets the market's needs, but also reinforces the brand's identity and story.

CUSTOMER FEEDBACK AND ARCHETYPES

Integrating customer feedback is essential to maintaining brand relevance and resonance, especially when it comes to aligning and refining the expression of your brand archetype. This chapter discusses how to collect, analyze, and apply customer feedback to enhance your archetype representation and ensure your brand stays connected with its target audience.

COLLECTING CUSTOMER FEEDBACK

Feedback collection methods:

- **Satisfaction surveys:** Use online or in-person surveys to ask customers directly how they perceive the brand archetype and its manifestations in products or services.

- **Focus groups:** Conduct focus group sessions to gain deeper insights into customers' perceptions, interpretations, and emotions regarding the brand archetype.

- **Social media monitoring:** Analyze comments and discussions about the brand on social media to capture public opinion and identify possible areas for improvement.

Integrating feedback into events and experiences:

- Host engagement events where customers can experience the brand archetype in action and provide real-time feedback.

ANALYZING FEEDBACK

Identifying patterns and trends:

- Use analytical tools to process the collected feedback and identify patterns or trends that indicate how the archetype is being received.

Assessment of archetype coherence:

- Determine whether the archetype is being perceived as intended and whether the manifestation of the archetype is aligned with the brand identity and values.

Feedback-based adjustments:

- If feedback indicates a disconnect between customer perception and brand intent, consider adjustments to communication, marketing, or even product offerings.

IMPLEMENTING CHANGES BASED ON FEEDBACK

Modifications to the product or service:

- Adjust products or services to better reflect the archetype, based on specific feedback about functionality, design, or user experience.

Improving marketing campaigns:

- Refine marketing campaigns to reinforce aspects of the archetype that resonate positively with audiences or revise messages that are causing confusion or negative reception.

Transparent communication:

- Communicate openly with customers about how their feedback is being used to improve the brand, reinforcing the brand image as attentive and responsive to customer needs and perceptions.

Customer feedback is a powerful tool for fine-tuning the expression of your brand archetype. By actively engaging with your audience and responding to their insights and needs, you can ensure that your brand archetype continues to evolve in ways that strengthen your connection with consumers and support sustainable brand growth.

TEAM BUILDING AND ARCHETYPES

Alignment between brand archetypes and internal teams is critical to ensuring that everyone within the organization understands, represents, and reinforces the brand vision in their daily interactions and strategic decisions. This chapter explores how archetypes can be used to build and develop teams that effectively and cohesively advance the brand's culture and goals.

UNDERSTANDING THE INFLUENCE OF ARCHETYPES ON TEAM BUILDING

Selection of talents aligned with the archetype:

- When recruiting new team members, consider how candidates' individual characteristics align with your brand archetype. For example, for a brand that embraces the Caregiver archetype, candidates with strong empathy and interpersonal skills may be a particular fit.

Developing archetype-based team culture:

- Cultivate a team culture that reflects the brand archetype. This can include work practices, team rituals, and activities that reinforce the archetype's values, such as collaborative brainstorming sessions for a Creator archetype, or outdoor team-building activities for the Explorer.

IMPLEMENTATION OF ARCHETYPE-BASED TRAINING

Personalized training:

- Develop training programs that help team members deeply understand the brand archetype and how it should influence their work. This can include workshops, simulations, and immersion sessions.

Performance evaluation aligned with archetypes:

- Incorporate performance reviews that consider how individuals contribute to the expression of the brand archetype in their roles. This helps keep everyone focused and aligned with the brand's goals.

STRENGTHENING LEADERSHIP WITH ARCHETYPES

Leaders as ambassadors of the archetype:

- Ensure that team leaders and managers exemplify the brand archetype in their actions and decisions. They should be seen as role models of the archetype, inspiring their teams to adopt and promote these values in their work.

Strategic decisions inspired by archetypes:

- Use the brand archetype to guide strategic decisions, from product development to marketing and operations strategies. Leaders who understand and apply the archetype can ensure that the brand remains consistent and relevant.

MEASURING THE IMPACT OF ARCHETYPES ON TEAM PERFORMANCE

Continuous feedback:

- Establish a continuous feedback system where team members can express how the archetype influences their work and suggest improvements.

Impact analysis:

- Conduct regular analyses to measure how integrating the archetype into team formation affects performance, job satisfaction, and overall team effectiveness.

Using archetypes to build and develop teams not only strengthens internal culture, but also ensures that the brand is represented consistently and powerfully across all facets of the organization. By investing in aligning archetypes with teams, companies can maximize brand consistency, employee motivation, and market success.

ARCHETYPES IN ADVERTISING

Advertising is a vital field for brand expression, and the use of archetypes can profoundly influence how advertising messages are received by audiences. This chapter discusses how archetypes can be used effectively in advertising campaigns to capture brand essence, reinforce brand identity, and engage consumers in meaningful ways.

INTEGRATING ARCHETYPES INTO ADVERTISING STRATEGY

Definition of key messages:

- Each archetype has unique attributes that can be highlighted in advertising messages. For example, a Hero archetype might focus on resilience and courage, while a Sage might focus on knowledge and confidence.

Selection of suitable media:

- Choose channels that best amplify the archetype. For example, social media might be a great fit for the Jester, with fun, viral campaigns, while the Caregiver might benefit from more engaging and personal formats, such as videos or podcasts that highlight real-life client stories.

Creation of visual and textual content:

- Develop content that visually and textually reflects the archetype. This includes the choice of colors, images, body language in visual ads and the tone of voice in texts.

EXAMPLES OF EFFECTIVE CAMPAIGNS BASED ON ARCHETYPES

Explorer Campaigns:

- A brand that embraces the Explorer archetype could create a campaign centered around adventure and discovery, perhaps promoting travel products or outdoor experiences.

Lover's Advertising:

- For a brand that identifies with the Lover archetype, advertising could focus on passion and emotional engagement, using rich, seductive imagery and messaging that speaks directly to consumers' emotional desires.

MEASURING THE EFFICACY OF ADVERTISING CAMPAIGNS

Engagement and conversion analysis:

- Monitor metrics such as views, dwell time, click-through rates, and conversion rates to assess the direct impact of archetype-based campaigns.

Brand perception research:

- Conduct research to understand how campaigns affect brand perception. This is particularly useful to check whether the archetype attributes are being communicated effectively.

Customer Feedback:

- Collect feedback directly from consumers to gain insights into how advertising is perceived and which aspects resonate most with them.

Using archetypes in advertising not only helps to strengthen a brand's identity, but also creates a deeper, more emotional connection with the audience. When executed well, advertising campaigns that use archetypes not only capture attention, but also build consumer loyalty by consistently reinforcing the brand's core values.

WORKSHOPS AND TRAININGS ON ARCHETYPES

For an archetype strategy to be effectively implemented and sustained over time, it is crucial that all teams within the organization understand and know how to apply these concepts in their day-to-day branding. Workshops and training are essential tools for disseminating this knowledge and engaging teams. This chapter explores how to organize and conduct effective archetype workshops, ensuring that participants not only understand the chosen archetype, but also how it should influence their work.

PLANNING WORKSHOPS ON ARCHETYPES

Goal setting:

- Clarify what you hope to achieve with the workshop. Goals might include increasing understanding of the archetypes, exploring how they apply to different areas of the brand, or developing ideas to better align team actions with the brand archetype.

Audience selection:

- Determine who should participate. This can range from senior leadership, who need to understand how archetypes influence strategic decisions, to marketing, product and sales teams, who need to apply the concept to product development and promotion.

Content development:

- Create materials that are informative and interactive. Presentations should include an explanation of what archetypes are, the specific archetype of the brand, and practical examples of how it can be applied.

WORKSHOP EXECUTION

Introduction to archetypes:

- Start with a basic introduction to what archetypes are and why they are important for branding. This is crucial to ensure that all participants have a common knowledge base.

Discussion of practical cases:

- Present case studies from within and outside the company, showing how the archetypes have been successfully implemented. This helps to illustrate the applicability of the concepts in a concrete way.

Interactive activities:

- Include interactive exercises, such as creating advertising campaigns or developing product ideas that reflect the archetype. This not only reinforces learning, but also stimulates creativity and engagement among participants.

Feedback and discussion:

- Encourage feedback and discussion during the workshop. This can provide valuable insights into how the team perceives the archetype and their suggestions for better integrating it into daily work.

EVALUATION AND FOLLOW-UP

Workshop evaluation:

- At the end of the workshop, collect feedback from participants to assess the effectiveness of the training and identify areas that may need further development or clarification.

Action plan:

- Develop an action plan based on the insights and feedback received during the workshop. This may include specific steps teams need to take to better align their work with the brand archetype.

Recycling sessions:

- Plan regular refresher sessions to revisit archetype concepts and discuss new ideas and approaches. Continually evolving the understanding and application of archetypes is critical to keeping the strategy dynamic and relevant.

Archetype workshops and trainings are essential to empower teams to understand and effectively implement the brand archetype strategy within their respective functions. With careful planning and execution, these trainings can transform the way internal teams perceive and contribute to the brand narrative, strengthening corporate culture and internal cohesion.

IMPLEMENTING A WINNING ARCHETYPE STRATEGY

After exploring in depth the various aspects of how brand archetypes can influence and improve different areas of business and communication, this final chapter brings together all the lessons learned and outlines an action plan for implementing a winning archetype strategy. Here, we will summarize best practices and outline the essential steps to ensure your archetype strategy is successful and delivers lasting results.

RECAPING KEY POINTS

Choosing the correct archetype:

- Select an archetype that authentically resonates with your brand's mission, vision and values. The right choice is essential to ensure a genuine connection with your audience.

Integration into all aspects of the brand:

- Incorporate the archetype into all areas of the brand, from product development to marketing, internal communications and customer experience.

Staff education and engagement:

- Ensure that all teams within the organization understand the archetype and how it should influence their day-to-day responsibilities.

Continuous monitoring and adaptation:

- Implement a continuous feedback system to monitor how the archetype is being perceived by the public and internal teams. Be ready to make adjustments as needed to keep the strategy relevant and effective.

ACTION PLAN FOR IMPLEMENTATION

Internal release:

- Start with an internal rollout of the archetype to the entire company, using workshops and training materials to ensure consistent understanding across the organization.

Aligned marketing campaigns:

- Develop and launch marketing campaigns that clearly communicate the archetype to the audience. Use stories, visuals, and messaging that consistently reinforce the chosen archetype.

Archetype-based performance assessment:

- Establish key performance indicators (KPIs) that help measure the archetype's impact on sales, customer engagement, and brand perception.

Regular reviews:

- Schedule regular reviews of the archetype strategy to assess its effectiveness and make strategic adjustments. Consider the current market environment, customer feedback, and internal innovations.

Implementing a successful brand archetype strategy requires more than just choosing an archetype and applying it superficially. It requires deep and thoughtful integration across all aspects of your brand, effective communication, and ongoing commitment from all teams involved. With careful planning, diligent execution, and ongoing monitoring, an archetype strategy can not only differentiate your brand in the marketplace, but also create a lasting and meaningful connection with your audience.

By following the steps outlined in this book, your brand will be equipped to implement an archetype strategy that not only authentically communicates who you are, but also continually delights, engages, and inspires your target audience.

CHECKLIST FOR EVALUATION OF ARCHETYPES IN EXISTING BUSINESSES

This bonus chapter provides a detailed checklist for companies that already have an archetype strategy in place. The goal is to ensure that the archetype is being applied effectively and to identify areas where improvements can be made to strengthen the brand's connection with its customers. This checklist serves as a diagnostic and optimization tool to ensure the coherence and effectiveness of your brand's archetype strategy.

ALIGNMENT WITH THE COMPANY'S MISSION AND VISION:

- Does the chosen archetype still reflect the company's mission and vision?

- Is there congruence between the brand values and the characteristics of the archetype?

CONSISTENCY IN BRAND COMMUNICATION:

- Is the archetype clearly reflected in all brand communications, including marketing, advertising, social media and internal communications?

- Have recent campaigns remained consistent with the archetype?

CUSTOMER PERCEPTION AND RECEPTION:

- How do customers perceive the brand archetype? Do they identify and react positively to it?

- Is there market research or customer feedback that indicates the archetype's effectiveness in establishing an emotional connection?

INTERNAL INTEGRATION AND TEAM COMMITMENT:

- Do internal teams understand and are committed to the archetype?

- Can employees identify how their roles contribute to the expression of the brand archetype?

IMPACT ON BUSINESS RESULTS:

- Has the use of the archetype positively impacted business outcomes such as sales, customer retention, or brand awareness?

- Are there metrics or performance indicators that demonstrate the success of the archetype strategy?

FEEDBACK AND ADAPTATION:

- Does the brand have mechanisms to collect and analyze ongoing feedback on how the archetype is received?

- Are there processes in place to adapt and refine the archetype based on changes in the market or consumer preferences?

TRAINING AND DEVELOPMENT:

- Does the company provide regular training to ensure that all team members understand and can apply the archetype in their work?

- Do new employees receive guidance on the importance of the archetype in the company's culture and strategy?

USING THE CHECKLIST

This checklist should be reviewed periodically to ensure that your archetype implementation remains relevant and effective. It can be used in team meetings, strategic reviews, or during planning sessions to assess and direct your brand strategy. Adjustments based on the answers to these questions can help you further align your brand with your chosen archetype, strengthening your brand identity and deepening your connection with your audience.

This resource is designed to help business leaders keep their brands dynamic, relevant, and deeply connected with their customers through the power of archetypes.

60-DAY ACTION PLAN FOR IMPLEMENTING ARCHETYPES IN NEW BUSINESSES

For new businesses, establishing a strong brand foundation from the start is crucial. This bonus chapter provides a detailed action plan for implementing brand archetypes into a new business over 60 days, ensuring a coherent and impactful brand strategy from launch.

DAYS 1-10: CHOOSING AND DEFINING THE ARCHETYPE

- **Archetype research:** Identify which archetype best aligns with the business's vision and core values. Consider factors such as the company's mission, target market, and competitive edge.

- **Archetype Strategy Definition:** Develop a detailed description of how the archetype will influence all aspects of the brand, including tone of voice, personality, and core values.

DAYS 11-20: BRAND IDENTITY DEVELOPMENT

- **Creation of visual identity:** Develop visual brand elements such as logo, color palette and typography that reflect the chosen archetype.

- **Branding materials:** Prepare all necessary branding materials, such as business cards, letterhead, and packaging, that consistently communicate the archetype.

DAYS 21-30: WEBSITE DEVELOPMENT AND ONLINE PRESENCE

- **Website construction:** Develop a website that visually incorporates the content and brand archetype.

- **Social media presence:** Establish profiles on relevant social networks and prepare a content plan that reflects the brand archetype.

DAYS 31-40: MARKETING AND COMMUNICATION PLANNING

- **Marketing strategy:** Develop a marketing strategy that uses the archetype to define the communications approach, including advertising, promotions, and partnerships.

- **Launch plan:** Plan a launch event or campaign that introduces the brand and its archetype to the market in an impactful way.

DAYS 41-50: TEAM TRAINING

- **Archetype workshops:** Hold workshops to train your team on the brand archetype, ensuring everyone understands how it should be communicated and experienced in their roles.

- **Archetype integration:** Ensure that all internal operations, from customer service to product management, are aligned with the archetype.

DAYS 51-60: LAUNCH AND MONITORING

- **Brand Launch:** Execute the launch event or start the market introduction campaign.

- **Monitoring and adjustments:** Start monitoring your brand's performance in terms of audience engagement, feedback, and sales. Adjust your strategies as needed to ensure that the archetype is being effectively communicated and received.

This 60-day action plan provides a detailed roadmap for new businesses to effectively implement a brand archetype, ensuring that all facets of the business are aligned from the start. Following this plan will not only help build a coherent and compelling brand, but it will also facilitate a deeper and more meaningful connection with your target audience, laying a solid foundation for future growth.

As we turn the final page of this journey together, I sincerely hope that the learnings shared here have touched your heart and sparked new perspectives. If this book has brought you any value, I kindly ask that you take a few moments to leave a review on Amazon. Your words not only help me grow and hone my craft, but they also guide other readers in their quests for knowledge and inspiration. Your opinion is a valuable gift, both for me and for the community of readers looking for stories that transform. I sincerely thank you for sharing this journey with me and I hope we can meet again in the pages of a new adventure.

REGINALDO OSNILDO

Hello, I'm Reginaldo Osnildo, an author and innovator in the areas of sales, technology, and communication strategies. My experience ranges from academia, as a professor and researcher at the University of Southern Santa Catarina, to practice as a strategist at Grupo Catarinense de Rádios. With a PhD in sales narratives and digital convergence, and a master's degree in storytelling and social imaginary, I bring to my readers a unique fusion of theory and practice. My goal is to provide knowledge in simple, practical, and didactic language, encouraging direct application in personal and professional life.

Yours sincerely

Reginaldo Osnildo

www.ingramcontent.com/pod-product-compliance
Lightning Source LLC
Chambersburg PA
CBHW071519220526
45472CB00003B/1076